What are trees and what are conifers?

In this guide, trees mean perennial woody plants having a single trunk growing out of the soil and more than two metres high. If a number of main woody branches grow from ground level, the plant is called a bush. These and other differences between trees and bushes are not strictly scientific but more or less arbitrary. For example there are many species which, depending on their habitat, grow either as a tree or a bush (eg Thuya and Juniper).

The term conifer is actually a popular expression and means trees which usually remain green throughout the year and have small narrow needles or scales instead of leaves. Botanically, this group are classed as gymnosperms. They are at a 'lower' stage of evolutionary development than the angiosperms, which are a more numerous and successful group. Angiosperms include deciduous trees and other flowering plants.

In gymnosperms the seed is not surrounded by an ovary but lies 'naked' on a scale. The flowers are single sex, ie either male or female. They usually grow on the same plant or actually on the same branch, though spatially separate. Such plants are called *monoecious*. In the Yew and the Juniper, to give two examples, the sexes are actually on different individual plants, ie they are *dioecious*.

The flowers are always without petals and therefore often very inconspicuous.

The needle or scale-like leaves do not drop in winter but last several years. As always there are exceptions, such as the Larch. This tree sheds its needles in autumn and grows new ones in spring.

Hints on use

To help in recognising conifers, this guide contains two additional aids:

● **Identification from the shape or arrangement of needles or scale-leaves:** Using the Table on page 7 (Identifying conifers from their needles) you can quickly pick out the most likely conifer genera unless they belong to those rare groups not listed in the guide. You will also find where the representative species of the genus are illustrated and described.

As a glance at the Identification Table will show, the selection in the fifth section is particularly large. This includes genera which are very similar to one another and it is at this point (or earlier) that the layman will always ask 'What is the difference between firs and spruces?' If you don't know the answer, read the description of the spruce on page 48.

● **Identification from cones or fruits:** This is a useful additional aid in recognising a conifer. Anyone who succeeds in finding a cone under his tree or picking one within reach, will probably have his doubts settled by the pictures of cones on pages 8 to 11. Under the pictures, you will find the page where the tree is illustrated and described in the guide. Fir-cones are not included, because they are less useful for identification, since fir-cones do not fall from the tree in one piece and they also usually grow near the tree-top out of reach. You will find all the cones, on a small scale, alongside the colour pictures and descriptions of trees in the species descriptions. Fir-cones are also shown there, for the sake of botanical completeness.

The cones are shown mainly in the closed state, ie their appearance when not quite ripe and hanging on the tree or when they have fallen in moist weather. In dry weather the cone scales spread out, thus completely altering their appearance. However, dried cones can easily be converted to their original state by placing in water; they will have re-closed within an hour.

Identifying conifers from their needles

Description of shape	Needles and shoot	May be a	Pages
Needles grow in groups of 2, 3 or 5 from a common leaf sheaf		Pine	62–79
Needles in thick bunches on older branches (young shoots have uniform covering of needles)		Larch, Cedar	22–79
Needles in two opposite rows, on side-shoots, not on the upward-growing shoots		Yew	12–13
Needles in threes like a Mercedes star, around the shoot		Juniper	20–21
Needles in spiral or brush shape or a number of rows around the shoot		Fir, Spruce, Hemlock, Douglas Fir, Wellingtonia, Japanese Cedar	30–61
Needles are mainly scaly. The scales overlap like roof tiles		Cypress, Lawson's Cypress, Thuya	14–19

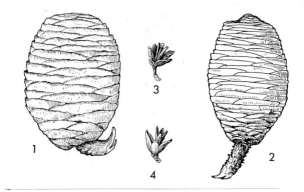

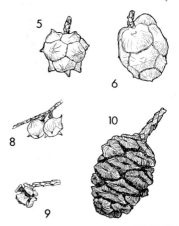

1. Cedar of Lebanon, *Cedrus libani* (p. 26)
2. Atlantic Cedar, *Cedrus atlantica* (p. 24)
3. White Cedar, *Thuja occidentalis* (p. 18)
4. Western Red Cedar, *Thuja plicata* (p. 19)
5. Smooth Arizona Cypress *Cupressus glabra* (p. 15)

6. Italian Cypress, *Cupressus sempervirens* (p. 14)
7. Douglas Fir, *Pseudotsuga menziesii* (p. 60)
8. Nootka Cypress, *Chamaecyparis nootkatenis* (p. 16)
9. Lawson's Cypress, *Chamaecyparis lawsoniana* (p. 16)
10. Wellingtonia, *Sequoiadendron giganteum* (p. 30)

8

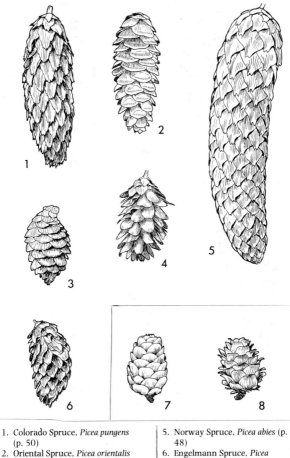

1. Mountain Pine, *Pinus mugo* (p. 64)
2. Macedonian Pine, *Pinus peuce* (pp. 70–79), normally longer
3. Austrian Pine, *Pinus nigra* (p. 66)
4. Scots Pine, *Pinus sylvestris* (p. 62)
5. Weymouth Pine, *Pinus strobus* (p. 70)
6. Yew, 7. Arolla 68)
8. Japanese Red Cedar, *Cryptomeria japonica* (p. 32)

10

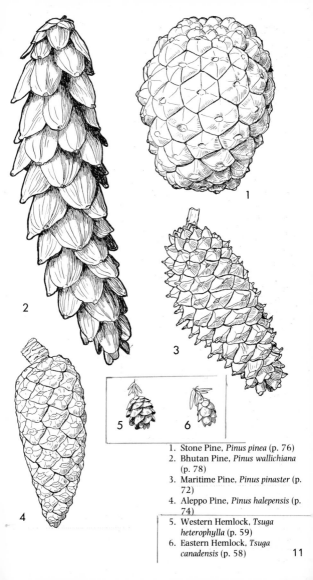

11

Yew

Taxus baccata
Yew Family (*Taxaceae*)

The characteristic features of the Yew are the strikingly dark
needles and the fact that it grows readily in the shade of higher
trees, either individually or in small groups, preferring limy
soil. The Yew is native through large parts of the Northern
Hemisphere. Its hard reddish-brown, very tough wood was
formerly used to make bows and cross-bows. (The Latin name
Taxus means bow.) Nowadays the wood is used for furniture.
The Yew can live over 2000 years. In mythology it is the tree
of death, and even nowadays it is planted in cemeteries, as
well as in parks. Since the Middle Ages, natural stands in
Europe have been losing ground, and consequently the tree is
nowadays protected in many countries. The needles and seeds
are very poisonous. There are numerous cultivars, which
differ from type as regards needle colour or shape of growth.

Growth: Very old trees are up to 20 m high, but most are
much lower. The shape varies, often with irregular crown and
short gnarled trunk, the branches growing out from close
above the ground. A bush form is quite common. **Bark:**
Reddish-brown purple, thin and skin-like, flaking. **Needles:**
soft, 2–4 cm long, flat, linear, with an abrupt sharp point.
Dark green, shiny on top, with marked centre rib, underside

Yew (*Taxus baccata*) with particularly regular growth.

yellow or grey-green and furrowed (without stripes). The needles are arranged in a spiral around upward-tending shoots, whereas on side shoots they are in two lines. **Flowers:** The Yew is dioecious. **Fruit:** Nut-like seeds surrounded by a red cup-shaped false berry or aril. Hence the Latin name *baccata* = with berries.

Shoots from a female tree with a fruit (aril). 13

Italian Cypress
Cupressus sempervirens
Cypress Family (*Cupressaceae*)

The striking dark columns of Cypresses are an essential part of gardens and parks in southern landscapes. This tree originally came from Persia, Asia Minor and Greece, but has now spread through the entire Mediterranean area. The Italian Cypress can live over 2000 years (*sempervirens* means with eternal life). In the second millennium BC, it was already sacred in Iran because of its flame shape. The Phoenicians used it to build ships, whereas Romans and Greeks used it for temple doors, memorial tablets and coffins. The very hard, dense wood is valued by cabinet-makers. (See page 16 for possible confusion with Thuya, False Cypresses and Junipers.)

Growth: Very narrow, almost columnar. **Trunk:** Up to 20 m high, thickly branching, bottom part bare. In the horizontal form, the branches project horizontally. **Bark:** Thin, grey-brown, cracked. **Shoots:** The branchlets are not flat but have a square cross-section and extend in all directions of space, ie not two-dimensionally. **Needles, scale-leaves:** Young plants bear needles, older plants only have scale-leaves, close-pressed, with a longitudinal furrow on the back, almost without scent, even when crushed. **Cones:** Lumpy egg-shaped, up to 4 cm long with pentagonal scales with a tiny

Italian Cypresses (*Cupressus sempervirens*) in a cemetery.

prickly point; first greenish then dark brown, finally grey-brown.

C. macrocarpa, *C. glabra* (picture of cone on page 8), *C. torulosa*, *C. lusitanica* are other species of Cypress which are mainly found in mild areas; some are broader with rounded top.

Cypress branch with last year's cone.

Lawson's Cypress
Chamaecyparis lawsoniana
Cypress Family (*Cupressaceae*)

Lawson's or False Cypresses can easily be mistaken for Thujas or True Cypresses, or even with some species of Juniper. They are often slender and conical. The layman will find it easiest to distinguish them by their cones or fruits; in False Cypresses they are spherical and small whereas Thuja cones are small but cup-shaped and true Cypress cones are lumpy egg-shaped and larger (1–4 cm). The similar Juniper species bear pseudo-berries. Lawson's Cypress was imported from Oregon, North-West USA in the mid-19th century and has now become very widespread in Europe, particularly in gardens and parks. The wood is yellowish, strong, durable, pleasant-smelling and of commercial value. There is a very large number of cultivars (about 130), which are difficult to identify except through acquaintance. They differ from the type described here in colour, shape of branches and general habit.

Growth: Narrow and conical, up to 30 m high, with branches down to the ground when free-standing. **Trunk:** Often forked, short horizontally-projecting branches.

Bark: Initially smooth and dark brown and green, later reddish and torn into long vertical strips. **Shoots:** First green,

Left and centre: Lawson's Cypress (*Chamaecyparis lawsoniana*).

later reddish-brown. They turn into flat 'branchlets' spreading in a single plane and covered with scale-leaves. These have a translucent oil gland in the middle (hold them up to the light) and are dark green above and paler underneath. The scale-leaves at the edge have a projecting tip. **Cones:** Spherical, numerous, about 8 mm across, initially green and blue-white pruinose, later purple-brown; the cone scales have small bumps. *C. obtusa*, *C. nootkatensis* (picture of cone on page 8) and *C. pisifera* are other species of False Cypress frequently planted in Europe; they, too, are found in many cultivars.

Branch with this year's and last year's cones.

White Cedar
Thuja occidentalis
Cypress Family (*Cupressaceae*)

There are six *Thuya* species, all from North America or East Asia. *T. occidentalis* has long been planted in Europe (since 1550) and is now a traditional part of our parks and gardens. There are now a large number of garden varieties, varying in colour, shape or branch and habit. The tree is undemanding and can be pruned at will, and is therefore often used in evergreen hedges. It is also called Arbor Vitae or Tree of Life, which is connected with the medicinal use of Thuya Oil obtained from the branches.

Growth: Narrow and conical with erect branch on top, height up to 20 m. **Trunk:** Often multi-stemmed, with branches down to ground. **Bark:** Grey-brown, torn into narrow strips. **Shoots:** Branching in one plane, branchlets are pressed flat. **Scale-leaves:** Close-packed like roof tiles. Dark green and dull glossy on top, pale green and dull underside; resinous fruity smell when crushed. The scales have clearly visible (translucent) oil glands on their wide side. **Cones:** About 1 cm across, egg-shaped, first greenish, then brown and spreading apart like a cup in the second year.

Western Red Cedar *Thuja plicata*
This species likewise comes from North America; it occurs not

A group of White Cedars (*Thuja occidentalis*).

only in parks and gardens but also in forests, owing to its wood. *T. plicata* can live for up to 800 years; its habit is very similar to *T. occidentalis*. The most striking differences are:

Growth: Wider top when old, height up to 40 m. **Trunk:** Widened at base. **Bark:** Dark red-brown. **Shoots:** Like *T. occidentalis*. **Scale-leaves:** Bright green on top, like shiny lacquer, whitish underside, often without oil-glands, very fruity smell. **Cones:** Like *T. occidentalis* (picture, page 8).

Typical two-dimensional branching. Last year's cones.

Juniper
Juniperus communis
Cypress Family (*Cupressaceae*)

The Juniper grows readily in sunny dry areas and is native in most of the northern temperate zone. Numerous cultivated varieties are frequently found in gardens. The Juniper can live for up to 800 years. Its dense, tough but soft wood is often used for turned work and also for walking-sticks and whip-handles. The smoke from its dried branches drives away evil spirits, according to popular belief, and also improves bacon and sausages cured in it. Juniper berries are found both in the kitchen and at the chemist's and, not least, they are used to prepare the various types of gin. The Common Juniper is dioecious.

Growth: Tree or bush, columnar, up to 8 m high. **Trunk:** Branches from ground upwards. **Needles:** The Common Juniper has needles only, not scale-leaves or both, as with other Juniper species. The needles grow in threes around the shoot, are stiff and prickly, do not end in an elongated ridge hanging from the shoot, are up to 15 mm long, boat-shaped, grey-green, and with a broad whitish stripe on top. **Fruit:** Cones or 'berries', spherical, 7–9 mm across, greenish then blue-black and bluish pruinose.

Juniper (*Juniperus communis*) in natural habitat.

Blue Chinese Juniper. *Juniperus squamata* Meyeri
This is a cultivar of *squamata*, which comes from the Central Asian mountains and is frequently planted in our gardens. Typical features: Blue-grey colour. **Needles:** Likewise in threes around shoot, prickly and stiff, up to 7 mm long, bent, blue-green on top, blue-white underneath. **Fruit:** Berry-like cones, first red-brown then black.

Branch with berry-like cones on a female tree.

European Larch
Larix decidua
Pine Family (*Pinaceae*)

A stately tree with conical crown. Its habitat is the Alps and Carpathians, where it grows in particular splendour, up to the tree limit. It can live for up to 600 years. Often planted as an ornamental tree, but also used in forestry. The wood is very durable and used particularly for building and tools. In autumn the leaves become shiny yellow and fall.

Growth: Straight trunk with erect top up to 35 m high, lower half often bare of branches. The branches are horizontal, the lower ones somewhat drooping. **Shoots:** Yellowish in first year. **Needles:** Growing individually on long-shoots, in bunches on short-shoots. They are soft, 10–30 mm long, light green (never bluish), grey-greenish underside. **Flowers:** The female flowers are crimson little cones. **Cones:** Red-brown, egg-shaped, up to 4 cm long, cone-scales not rolled back.

Japanese Larch *Larix kaempferi*
In habit similar to *L. decidua*. The Latin name commemorates the German scientist and traveller Engelbert Kämpfer, who lived in Japan from 1690 to 1692 and described the country and its people. The Japanese Larch has become established in many parts of Europe, not only in parks but also in forests. At

European Larch (*Larix decidua*) in the Alps.

places where the air and ground moisture are sufficient, it is superior to the European Larch. The wood has the same uses as *L. decidua*.

Growth: Branches not drooping, upward-growing top branches. The crown is wide in old trees. **Shoots:** Reddish orange-brown in first year, often pruinose. **Needles:** Blue-green on both sides, 20–35 mm long, soft, two grey stripes on underside, otherwise like *L. decidua*. **Cones:** Brown, almost spherical, up to 4 cm long, cone-scales rolled back at edge (picture on page 9).

Short-shoots and last year's cones.

Atlantic Cedar

Cedrus atlantica
Pine Family (*Pinaceae*)

Cedars have certain similarities to Larches, in general habitat and in the arrangement of needles, which grow in thick bunches on short-shoots. Like Larches, Cedars are mountain trees. They are native in mountainous areas in the Mediterranean region and Asia: Atlas, Lebanon, Taurus, Antitaurus, Cyprus, Afghanistan, and the Himalayas. The Atlantic Cedar, which comes from the Atlas mountains in North Africa where it forms thick woods at altitudes of up to 1000 metres, has been planted as an ornamental tree since the mid-19th century, mainly in the mild climate of South Europe. It also, however, flourishes in sheltered sites in Central Europe (eg in Germany at Lake Constance, in the Rhineland and in Rugen). It is planted in many British gardens. The Glauca form in particular, with its intense blue needles, has proved particularly robust and grows in places unsuitable for other Cedar species or forms. Cedars (there are three main species and a number of cultivars) are distinguished mainly by their needles, since the growth is often so individual that it is very difficult to recognise a tree from its external shape, particularly old trees (Cedar of Lebanon and Deodar, pages 26 and 28).

Growth: Up to 40 m high, loosely conical in youth with erect

Atlantic Cedar (*Cedrus atlantica*) in a park.

top branch, later irregular. **Trunk:** Often multi-stemmed when old; irregular branches growing steeply upward; the Glauca form is noticeable because of its bulky projecting branches. **Bark:** Grey and smooth when young, later somewhat cracked. **Shoots:** With thick hair, yellowish, side-shoots do not droop. **Needles:** 15–25 mm long, in bunches on short-shoots, growing individually on long-shoots, stiff and pointed, bluish-green (steel-blue in the case of Glauca). **Cones:** 5–7 cm long, barrel-shaped, with flat or hollowed tip, light green in first year, light brown in second year, erect; ripe cone falls from tree.

Shoots of blue-needled variety, *Cedrus atlantica* 'Glauca'.

Cedar of Lebanon
Cedrus libani
Pine Family (*Pinaceae*)

This tree with its widely projecting plate-like branches is often broader than high when full-grown. It originated from the Lebanon and Taurus mountains in Asia Minor, where it grows at altitudes up to 2000 m. Old trees in Lebanon have an estimated age of 2000 to 3000 years. In the first half of the 17th century the Cedar of Lebanon was brought to Europe and planted as an ornamental tree. Since it does not withstand winter everywhere, it flourishes mainly in the Mediterranean region, western France and southern England. In Germany it is found in mild areas in the Rhine Valley and around Lake Constance. Probably *Cedrus libani* is not the famous tree of antiquity, since its wood is soft and without the durability ascribed to Cedar. The ancient building-material probably came from various species of Juniper which were called Cedars. True Cedar wood, because of its pleasant smell, was used for incense, or for boxes and caskets for keeping precious objects. The chips and resin were used for embalming corpses. The name Cedar comes from the Greek 'Kedros'. The word originally denoted a species of Juniper, and was used for Cedar later. (Atlantic and Himalayan Cedar, pages 24 and 28.)

Cedar of Lebanon (*Cedrus libani*) in a park.

Growth: Up to 20 m high, initially conical with erect leading shoot, later with flat crown and spreading umbrella shape. **Trunk:** Multi-stemmed when old, branches projecting far to the side, spreading out in flat tables. **Shoots:** Sparse-haired. **Needles:** 15–30 mm long, in bunches in short-shoots, stiff, pointed, usually dark green and not bluish green as with *C. atlantica* and *C. deodara*. **Cones:** 8–12 cm long, flat or hollowed in front, firstly light green, later dark-brown with resin coating.

Long-shoots and short-shoots with bunches of needles.   27

Deodar

Cedrus deodara
Pine Family (*Pinaceae*)

The Deodar, unlike other Cedar species, has drooping branch-ends. This is particularly striking in younger trees; when old their habit is more similar to that of other Cedars, ie the Atlantic or Cedar of Lebanon. The tree comes from Afghanistan and the Himalayas, where it grows at altitudes up to 2000 m. It was regarded as sacred by the Hindus (the species name deodara comes from *deva-dáru*, the Sanskrit for divine tree). Owing to its decorative appearance it was introduced into Europe at the beginning of the 19th century and adorns gardens and parks, particularly in the Mediterranean area. In Central Europe it grows only in particularly favourable sites.

As before, it is extraordinarily difficult to tell species of Cedar apart. Old trees are often so similar in shape or so individualised and deviant from the norm that even the expert may be at a loss. Even needle lengths vary within one and the same species, and are therefore of little help in identification. Normally the deodar can be recognised from its drooping branch-ends and relatively long, soft needles (Atlantic and Cedar of Lebanon, pages 24 and 26).

Growth: Up to 20 m high (up to 50 m in its habitat); conical in youth, with drooping leading shoot, later with wide crown.

Deodar (*Cedrus deodara*).

Trunk: With horizontal branches, forming plates. **Shoots:** The young shoots have thick hair, the tips of side-shoots droop. **Needles:** 30–50 mm long in bunches on short-shoots, pointed but soft, bluish-green (as with *C. atlantica*). **Cones:** 8–12 cm long, barrel-shaped, with blunt non-pointed tip, initially bluish pruinose, later reddish-brown. There are about 10 cultivars including some with blue needles.

Typical drooping shoots at branch-ends.

Wellingtonia

Sequoiadendron giganteum
Swamp Cypress Family (*Taxodiaceae*)

There are two Big-Trees, *Sequoiadendron giganteum* described here, which is fairly resistant to winter in Central Europe, and *Sequoia sempervirens* or the Coast Redwood, which flourishes in warmer places. In its habitat, the Sierra Nevada in California, the Wellingtonia can grow up to 100 m, but the Coast Redwood, which also comes from California, can reach 110 m. *Sequoiadendron giganteum* can live for 3500 years. It was discovered in 1850 and the seeds very quickly reached England, the classic land of tree-lovers. The oldest trees are therefore about 130 years old and only 50 m high. Nowadays, *S. giganteum* also occurs in parks in Europe, where it has already reached a height of 30 m. It is also being experimentally planted in forests, but it has been found that in Europe wood from this tree, in contrast to America, is fairly soft and of little use.

Growth: Uniform, narrow and conical, usually with pointed crown but often rounded. **Trunk:** With very wide base up to about 2 m, then slimmer; side branches upward-growing near top, horizontal underneath and drooping below, but bent upwards at ends. **Bark:** Red and surprisingly thick, spongy and with deep cracks; can be gouged out by hand.

Two Wellingtonias (*Sequoiadendron giganteum*).

Shoots and branchlets: stiff, bent upwards at ends. **Needles:** In spirals round the entire shoot, 3–8 mm long, blue-green; they are appressed and look like long pointed scale-leaves having a projecting tip. **Cones:** Egg-shaped, 5–8 cm long, on long stalks; older cones lying under the tree are brown-black and only slightly open. The cone scales are wide, rhombic and bulbous. May be confused (needles, colour of trunk) with Japanese Cedar, *Cryptomeria japonica* (page 32).

Branch with upward-growing shoots.

Japanese Red Cedar
Cryptomeria japonica
Swamp Cypress Family (*Taxodiaceae*)

This conifer has a strikingly soft, rounded shape; even its top is rounded. It comes from China and from the mountains of Southern Japan, where it grows as a forest tree. In the mid-19th century the Japanese Red Cedar was planted in Europe, where various garden varieties are also cultivated. However, it flourishes only in sheltered, moist places. The Greek scientific name records the fact that the branches are concealed (by the needles). In its habitat, the Japanese Red Cedar is also planted in forests, since the straight, branch-free trunk is highly valued. It is now experimentally planted in our forests. In a Japanese Red Cedar forest, or even under single trees, there is a conspicuous ground covering of red, palm-sized dead branches. Like many other conifers, every few years the tree sheds not individual needles but entire side-shoots with their needle and cone-bearing twigs.

Trunk: Up to 40 m high, wide base, slimmer above, top branches are horizontal whereas lower branches are somewhat drooping but turn upwards further out. **Bark:** Reddish-brown, comes off in long strips. **Needles:** Hard, pointed, 5–12 mm long, sickle-shaped and bent towards shoot, bright green or yellow-green, with projecting ridge on underside, in five

Two Japanese Cedars (*Cryptomeria japonica*).

spiral rows around shoot. **Male flowers:** In thick panicles around branch-ends, often so numerous that the pollen stains the crown. **Cones:** Spherical, 2 cm across, on upwardly curved stalks; first greenish, then brown; each cone-scale has 4–6 points.

Shoots with this year's cones. Typical sickle-shaped needles.

Common Silver Fir

Abies alba
Pine Family (*Pinaceae*)

The Silver Fir is native in the mountains of Western, Central and Southern Europe, where it still grows at altitudes up to 2000 m. It can live up to 500 years. The species name alba means 'white', although it is not quite clear whether the colour refers to the white underside of the needles or the white-grey bark. Silver Fir wood is easy to work and used inter alia to make soundboards for musical instruments. There are some special garden forms of the Silver Fir, but the Christmas 'fir-tree' is usually a Spruce. The general difference between firs and spruces will be described on page 48.

Growth: Up to 50 m high, narrow, conical, with horizontal branches; the crown forms a flattish, forked top when old. **Bark:** White-grey, smooth with resin blisters in young trees, broken and rough when older. **Shoots:** Grey-brown, rough-haired, not furrowed. **Needles:** 15–30 mm long, flat, shiny, dark green on top, with two white stripes underneath, notched at apex, usually parted in a double row. The coat of needles varies widely, depending on situation and light. **Cones:** 10–16 cm long, erect as in all Fir species and not falling.

Group of Silver Firs (*Abies alba*) in natural habitat.

The **Giant Fir**, *Abies grandis*, is very similar. This Fir, which comes from the west coast of North America, grows almost 100 m high in its homeland; in Europe, where it has grown since the first half of the 19th century, it is not taller than the Silver Fir. It is planted in parks and also in forests owing to its rapid growth. It is not easy to distinguish from a Silver Fir. The Giant Fir can be recognised from the initially brownish-red, later dark brown bark and the longer needles (up to 60 mm), which are also parted in a double row, the upper row consisting of shorter needles.

Shoots with typical parted arrangement of needles.

Caucasian Fir
Abies nordmanniana
Pine Family (*Pinaceae*)

The Caucasian Fir is similar in growth to the Silver Fir initially conical but narrow and columnar when old. The tre comes from Asia Minor and the Western Caucasus where i forms thick forests at an altitude of 1000 to 2000 m an grows about 70 m high. About the middle of the 19th centur the Caucasian Fir was brought to Europe. Originally it wa planted in parks instead of the native Silver Fir, owing to it better growth and thicker needles. In some parts of Europe it i now planted in forests and increasing numbers are sold a Christmas trees. The tree requires high atmospheric humidit and does not tolerate city smoke and dust. There are som cultivars, eg a Glauca (bluish) and a dwarf and a droopin form.

Growth: Up to 30 m high, with branches down to the groun even when old, particularly when free-standing. **Trunk** Thick branches in regular whorls, somewhat upward tending. **Bark:** Initially dull, light grey and smooth, later dark grey and torn into thick plates. **Shoots:** Initially smooth an shining olive yellow, later pink-brown, occasionally hairy **Needles:** 20–35 mm long, with a longitudinal groove, blunt o notched at tip, leathery; shiny green above, with two whit

Caucasian Fir (*Abies nordmanniana*). Norway Spruces (*Picea abies*).

strips underneath; the needles grow around the shoot, less thick underneath than on top; they extend to the front – towards the branch tip; the needles have a somewhat fruity smell if crushed. **Cones:** 12–15 cm long and 5 cm across, erect, limited to the top zone, often very numerous; brown and resinous; the bracts are bent outwards and have a hooked projection. The difference from the Silver Fir is most clearly shown in the needles; they are shorter, closer together and not appreciably parted.

The wide needles grow all around the shoot.

Colorado Fir
Abies concolor
Pine Family (*Pinaceae*)

A very decorative tree, particularly when free-standing, with its grey-green coat of needles reaching to the ground. The Colorado Fir can easily be identified and recognised by a layman, because of its extraordinarily long needles, bent in a sickle shape upwards. The name Colorado Fir indicates the tree's habitat, which extends from South California, Utah and Colorado to Mexico. Since the end of the 19th century the tree has also been planted in Europe. The name *concolor* (Uniformly-coloured) refers to the colour of the needles, which is the same on both sides. In much of Britain it does not thrive, but is planted in gardens and parks, in Germany and other European countries. There are some cultivars, which differ in the colour, length and thickness of the needles, which are likewise curved.

Growth: Loosely conical; height up to 40 m; horizontal branches; free-standing trees have branches down to the ground. **Bark:** Grey, rough, with many resin blisters. **Shoots:** Grey-green when young, later grey-brown, glabrous. **Needles:** Dull grey-green to grey-blue on both sides, thick, leathery and soft with a green central rib underneath, 40 to 80 mm long and bent in a sickle-shape upwards; in two rows

Young Colorado Fir (*Abies concolor*) in a park.

on the shady side, thicker on the sunny side. **Cones:** Concentrated at tree top, about 10 cm long, first blue-green, later dull violet; as with all species of Fir, the cones remain on the tree and do not drop off.

The upwardly bent needles are typical.

Nikko Fir

Abies homolepis
Pine Family (*Pinaceae*)

The Nikko Fir has a typical kind of branch formation, from which it can be recognised in its habit – ie very thickly ramifying branches extending horizontally in plates. The habitat of the Nikko Fir is Japan. The seeds, brought to Europe in 1860, probably come from Nikko, the temple city in the nature reserve – hence the name of the tree. The scientific species name *homolepis* (with uniform scales) probably refers to the bark of the trunk. This beautiful, decorative Fir appears less frequently in our parks than on the continent, but tolerates town air better than many Firs.

Growth: Wide and conical, up to 40 m high; pointed top (flattened in the 'Umbellata' variety). **Trunk:** When young the branches extend upwards, later horizontally; free-standing trunks have branches down to the ground even when old. **Bark:** Initially light brownish and smooth, later grey and scaly. **Shoots:** Light yellow-brown and shiny, with deep furrows, not hairy. **Needles:** Very close-packed and stiff, with prominent longitudinal furrow, blunt at end, notched or two-pointed; shiny green top (as if varnished), with two white stripes underneath; the needles grow on thick green cushions, and are parted more strongly above the shoot and less so

Nikko Fir (*Abies homolepis* var. 'Umbellata').

underneath (V-shaped); Needles 20–30 mm at the side, only
10–20 mm long on top. **Cones:** Erect as with all Firs, and do
not fall; they are cylindrical, up to 9 cm long and 3 cm thick;
initially (before ripening) purple-violet, later brown; they are
present in surprising numbers, even on the lowest branches.
There is thus the opportunity to take hold of a cone instead of
just looking at it. If the unripe cones are light yellow instead of
purple-violet, the tree is *Abies homolepis* var. Umbellata (=
unbrella-shaped).

The needles are wide and notched in front.

Korean Fir
Abies koreana
Pine Family (*Pinaceae*)

This smallish tree is particularly suitable for gardens, since it takes up little space. In Korea, its homeland, it grows up to 15 m high, but scarcely reaches 10 m in Europe. This small stature when grown abroad is observable in other trees also. The Korean Fir was first brought to Europe in 1910, but soon became very popular owing to the decorative cones, which begin to form on very young plants. Trees not yet a metre in height can already bear the colourful cones. The Korean Fir makes few demands on site or ground; it is important for the soil to be sufficiently moist in autumn so that the tree survives the winter.

Growth: First conical, wide and dwarf-shaped; a fast-growing central shoot forms later. **Trunk:** The branches grow in whorls out of the trunk and rise slightly. **Bark:** Sprinkled with clearly visible raised places. These are bark pores or 'lenticels'. **Shoots:** Furrowed and very hairy, yellowish-red. **Needles:** Almost completely around the shoot, only 10 to 20 mm long, usually widened towards the tip, which is rounded or notched but pointed in the top part of the tree; the colour is shiny green on top, white with two chalky-white stripes underneath. The needles grow on a short stalk from the shoot. **Cones:**

Young Korean Fir (*Abies koreana*), already bearing cones.

Conspicuously violet or reddish-brown when unripe, barrel-shaped, 4–7 cm long, usually somewhat wider towards the tip; the bracts project and are folded back. Even young trees have large numbers of cones. When ripe they are brown to black.

The needles of the Korean Fir are strikingly short.

Noble Fir
Abies procera
Pine Family (*Pinaceae*)

One of the most beautiful Firs when it can grow free-standing. It comes from the west of North America (Oregon, Washington), where it grows in the mountains and is up to 80 m high. In continental Europe, where it was introduced in 1930, it has hitherto reached a height of only 20–30 m. Some taller British specimens are known. The Noble Fir is slim and conical and is found mainly as an ornamental tree, but is used in forestry in the West. The Latin name *procera* means long, high or slim. In addition to the standard type, the bluish variety Glauca is frequently planted.

Trunk: With branches down to the ground when free-standing; the lower branches droop considerably. **Bark:** Smooth, silver-grey with many transverse resin blisters, dark brown and with deep cracks when old. (The blisters contain thinly-liquid resin, and the same applies to other trees). **Shoots:** Brown-red, not furrowed, very hairy. **Needles:** Soft, 25–35 mm long, slightly furrowed, notched at tip, blue-green on top, with two narrow dull-white stripes underneath; needles close together; spread out flat (parted) on both sides underneath the shoot; the top row of needles is shorter, points to the front and is pressed against the shoot. **Cones:** Cylindri-

Young Noble Firs (*Abies procera*) in a young forest plantation.

cal, very large (15–25 cm long, 7–8 cm thick), first green, later purple-brown with pale green bracts.

The **Red Fir**, *Abies magnifica*, is very similar.
It comes from California and was introduced into Europe as early as 1850. In its homeland it grows to a height of 60–80 m, but reaches scarcely half this height in Europe. The Red Fir has a thick trunk, is narrow and conical and very regular in shape, like the Noble Fir. By contrast, however, *Abies magnifica* does not have resin blisters on younger trunks. The needles are also longer (up to 40 mm), stiff and not parted.

The needles spread out to the sides. 45

Veitch's Silver Fir
Abies veitchii
Pine Family (*Pinaceae*)

This Fir is somewhat similar to the Caucasian Fir as regards needles; for the layman the clearest distinguishing feature is the strikingly silver-white underside of the needles, which are twisted so far to the side or upwards that the tree appears frost-covered, particularly at the top. Veitch's Silver Fir, like many of our park trees, comes from Japan, where the climate is similar to that in Europe. It was first planted in Europe in 1879, in Veitch's wholesale English market garden – thus explaining the name. The tree can stand our winter and grows quickly during its first years – it is the fastest-growing species of *Abies*. This is probably the reason why it is occasionally considered for use in forestry.

Growth: Up to 25 m, regularly narrow and conical, still narrower in age and often with flat top. **Trunk:** Horizontal branches growing from very regular whorls. **Bark:** Strikingly light grey and smooth. There are clearly visible recesses under the place where the branches begin. **Shoots:** Yellowish or grey, with thick hair. **Needles:** Up to 25 mm long, soft, furrowed on top, blunt or notched at tip and narrowing into a stalk at the base; shiny green on top, with conspicuous silver-white stripes underneath; the needles are very close-packed,

Young Veitch's Fir (*Abies veitchii*).

xtend forwards or upwards and are partly twisted; those
under the shoot are bent to the side. **Cones:** 5–7 cm long,
ylindrical, first bluish or olive-green, later brown, erect;
ones grow already on young trees and are close-packed on
older trees.

typical wide chalk-white stripes on underside of needles.   47

Norway Spruce
Picea abies
Pine Family (*Pinaceae*)

The Norway Spruce has become progressively more wide spread in recent centuries and is now the most important forest tree in central Europe. It is native in the European mountains in the central and northern region. It can grow at altitudes of 2000 m, eg in the Engadine. Scarcely any other tree grows in so many different shapes, either natural or produced by cultivation – a fact which does not make it easy for the layman to recognise the Norway Spruce or its differences from other species. On the other hand, Spruces have an easily recognisable feature – the cones, which, unlike Firs, do not remain on the tree but fall in one piece. (Two other differences: Spruce needles grow on small bumps which remain on the branch after the needles have fallen; Fir needles grow directly on the branch and only leave a roundish scar. Spruce cones droop whereas Fir-cones remain erect on the branch.) The Norway Spruce lives for up to 500 years; its wood has a variety of uses. The genus name *Picea* is related to the Latin *pix* (pitch) and records the fact that pitch was formerly obtained from the resin of Norway and other Spruces.

Growth: Up to 50 m, pointed and conical. **Trunk:** Branches in whorls, pointing upward on top, drooping below, but up-tilted

Norway Spruce (*Picea abies*) in an Alpine meadow.

...at the end. **Bark:** Reddish with thin scales. **Shoots:** Reddish-yellow, glabrous or hairy. **Needles:** 10–25 mm long, straight or bent, with four sides, pointed, somewhat prickly, dark green on all sides, radially on erect shoots, parted underneath on horizontal shoots. **Cones:** 10–15 cm long, first green or reddish, later light brown. Rigid, firm scales, narrowing into a relatively pronounced tongue at the edge.

...pruce needles are often slightly curved.

Colorado Spruce

Picea pungens
Pine Family (*Pinaceae*)

The Colorado Spruce is one of the commonest ornamental trees in our gardens and parks. The particularly popular blue-shaped varieties are known under the general name Glauca, a term often used for conifer varieties and derived from the Latin *glaucus* (blue-grey/blue-green). Other varieties, green or blue, are dwarfs or have drooping branches. Sometimes this Spruce is also planted in forests. It comes from the south-west of North America (Rocky Mountains, Utah, Colorado), where it grows individually at altitudes up to 3300 m. The tree was brought to Europe about 1860. It is remarkably insensitive to smoke and city dust and undemanding as regards ground and position.

Growth: Height up to 30 m, conical, thickly covered. **Trunk:** Very thick underneath, horizontal branches, bending downwards in older trees, in thick regular whorls. **Bark:** Grey-brown when young, darker when old, with long deep furrows and coming off in small flakes. **Shoots:** *Glabrous*, first smooth and light brown, later brown and then blackish. **Needles:** 20-30 mm long, with four sides, rigid, terminating in a prickly point; distributed round the entire shoot; often somewhat sparser underneath. Colour: Dull green to silver-grey or blue.

Young Colorado Spruce, blue-green variety (*Picea pungens* 'Glauca').

rey, same colour on all four sides. **Cones:** 7–10 cm long, light rown, with very thin but stiff cone-scales with tapering ongue in front, toothed at end.

Similar species: **Dragon Spruce** (*P. asperata*) with paper-hin bark scales, shorter needles (10–18 mm) and brown-red ones, having leathery scales which are entire and not rolonged in front. Also the **Engelmann Spruce** (*P. ngelmannii*). It is planted in forests (in North Europe) as well s gardens and parks. The four-sided needles have white tripes on all four surfaces.

he needles of the Colorado Spruce are rigid and very harp (var. 'Glauca').

Serbian Spruce
Picea omorika
Pine Family (*Pinaceae*)

This Spruce can easily be recognised from its strikingl
narrow shape. When free-standing it is one of the mos
decorative conifers, with its narrow trunk and branche
hanging to the ground. It is native to Serbia and Bosnia i
southern Yugoslavia, where it grows on steep mountai
slopes and once covered the mountains up to 1500 m. Sinc
then the Serbian Spruce has declined considerably in it
homeland but is widespread in the rest of Europe. It is th
Spruce most commonly found in parks, cemeteries an
gardens. Apart from its decorative growth, it is often plante
in confined places. It will probably also be suitable for forestry
when enough experience is available. The wood grow
slowly, but the increase in length is considerable, particularl
in youth. 'Omorika' is the Serbian for 'Spruce'.

Growth: Up to 30 m high, very narrowly conical. **Trunk**
Thickened where branches begin, with recess underneath
horizontal branches, lower ones drooping and rising in
curve at the outside. **Bark:** Orange-brown, with paper-thi
scales, which later become hard and square. **Shoots:** Brown
hairy. **Needles:** 8–15 cm long, with four sides but pressed fla
together so as to produce a keel at top and bottom, sharp

Serbian Spruce (*Picea omorika*) in a park.

pointed (in young trees) or blunt with small tip (when older); shiny dark green on top, with two white stripes underneath; needles slightly bent, growing all around shoot, but occasionally somewhat parted on underside. The upper needles are bent upwards so that the white underside is visible. **Cones:** 3–5 cm long, pointed tip, dark-brown and black when young, shiny cinnamon brown when ripe; scales are stiff, wide and roundish, toothed at edge; even young trees have many cones.

The bent-back needles show the stripes underneath.   53

Sitka Spruce
Picea sitchensis
Pine Family (*Pinaceae*)

The Sitka Spruce comes from a narrow coastal region in western North America extending from Alaska to California including the islands of Vancouver and Sitka, which gives the Spruce its name. It grows there at altitudes up to 2000 m and forms dense stands with other conifers. In 1831 it was introduced to Europe by Douglas, a Scottish gardener. As its origin clearly shows, it is used to a cool, moist climate, and so flourishes best in our coasts, beside lakes and river-banks. When the site is suitable, as in western Britain, the Sitka Spruce is also planted in forests, since it grows quickly (the full-grown tree is usually higher and thicker than other Spruces) and its wood is excellent, light and tough and suitable as a building-material. It is now the most frequently planted forest tree in Britain. Otherwise the tree is found mainly in parks.

Growth: About 40 m high (over 60 m in its homeland), wide and conical, looser when old. **Trunk:** Branches in whorls horizontally projecting and upward-growing only in the upper part of the tree; a typical feature of older free-standing trees. Small needle-covered twigs grow from the branch-free regions of the trunk. **Bark:** Red-brown, initially thin, later

Two young Sitka Spruces (*Picea sitchensis*).

...aking. **Shoots:** Light yellowish to brownish, shiny, glabrous, ...urrowed and with a cushion of sharply projecting needles. **Needles:** 15–20 mm long, straight or bent, pressed together ...ut with four sides, hard, stiff with prickly tip; shiny dark ...reen with two white lines on top, with two bluish-white ...tripes underneath. The needles project obliquely to the front, ...nd grow on strong shoots around the twig; they are parted in ... V on the lower shoots. **Cones:** 5–8 cm long; cone-scales ...aper-thin but rigid, yellow-brown, round and flat in front.

...he curved, very sharp needles are typical.

Oriental Spruce

Picea orientalis
Pine Family (*Pinaceae*)

A stately conifer having branches reaching to the ground when free-standing. From a distance the Oriental Spruce cannot easily be distinguished from other Spruces. Seen close at hand, however, it can be very quickly recognised from its particularly short needles, which are also blunt (most Spruce species have sharp needles). Its habitat is the Caucasus and the Taurus mountains, where it forms large forests at altitudes of 2000 m. Although discovered in the 18th century, the Oriental Spruce was not brought to Europe and propagated until about 1840. It is found in our parks and gardens and occasionally in a cut hedge. It does not make any special demands on the ground and site and can even be planted in the shade, since the needles are not dropped there. It is cultivated in forests to a slight extent in some European countries (Belgium, Austria and Italy). There are also some cultivars (gold-coloured, dwarf and drooping forms).

Growth: Up to 30 m high (up to 60 m in its homeland), conical. **Trunk:** Branches close down to the ground, branches horizontal or upward-growing, tilted slightly upwards at end, in irregular whorls. **Bark:** Brown with few cracks, soon break off in small scales. **Shoots:** Light brown or whitish, hairy.

Oriental Spruce (*Picea orientalis*) on left, alongside *Picea omorika*.

Needles: Only 6–8 mm long with four sides, thick and stiff, rounded in front, dark green on all sides and looking as if varnished, without white stripes; extending forwards on top side of shoot, thus covering it. The needle cushions are very prominent. **Cones:** 6–9 cm long, elongated, first green to purple-red, later brown. Scales are wide and round with smooth edge.

Oriental Spruces have short needles with four sides.   57

Eastern Hemlock
Tsuga canadensis
Pine Family (*Pinaceae*)

A very decorative conifer with irregular habit and slightly drooping branches and twigs. It comes from eastern North America where it grows in cool, often rocky habitats, eg in moist canyons. The Eastern Hemlock was brought to Europe by 1740 and has now become widespread. It is usually found in gardens and parks; only occasionally in forests owing to the poor quality of its wood. It prefers moist, not too hot areas and also flourishes in semi-shade. The name Hemlock is apparently due to the smell of the leaves when crushed.

Growth: Up to 30 mm high, irregular, wide and conical. **Trunk:** With single stem in homeland, often multi-stemmed in central Europe; branches horizontal or rising obliquely irregularly positioned. **Shoots:** Light brownish, hairy. **Needles:** Only 5–15 mm long, soft, flat, blunt, not notched perceptibly serrated at edge, gradually tapering from base to tip; dark green and shiny on top, with two white stripes underneath, parted on shoot. **Cones:** Up to 2.5 cm long, egg-shaped, on short stalk, roundish scales, entire.

The **Western Hemlock**, *Tsuga heterophylla*, is very similar. It comes from western North America, from Alaska to Califor-

A full-grown Eastern Hemlock (*Tsuga canadensis*).

nia, and was brought to Europe in the middle of the 19th century, and grows in gardens and parks. *Heterophylla* means with varying leaves and relates to the different leaf lengths on the shoot, which also applies to *T. canadensis*. The most important difference is in the needles, which are of the same width from the base to the tip in the Western Hemlock. Also, the cones have no stalk (picture on page 11).

The needles of *Tsuga canadensis* are wider at the base than at the tip.

Douglas Fir
Pseudotsuga menziesii
Pine Family (*Pinaceae*)

The Douglas Fir is in fact neither Fir nor Spruce but a member of a separate genus, but has much in common with both; it looks like a wider Spruce and, like it, sheds its cones, but its needles have Fir characteristics since they grow directly on the shoot and when dropping or torn off leave only a round scar instead of a bump as in Spruces. The Latin name *Pseudotsuga* indicates certain resemblances to *Tsuga* (Hemlock), ie soft needles, which are often parted in two rows on young shoots. The Douglas Fir was native in Europe before the Ice Age, but then became extinct. In North America it survived in the North-West, from Canada to the southern Rocky Mountains and was again planted in Europe in the 18th century. The credit of having done this belongs to the Scottish gardener and botanish Douglas (1727). Since then the tree has been extensively planted in European forests and also in gardens and parks. The Douglas Fir can live up to 600 years; it grows quickly and yields valuable wood.

Growth: Up to 40 m high (up to 100 m in America), wide and conical. **Trunk:** Branches rising in youth, later horizontal, covered with drooping twigs, branches down to the ground when free-standing. **Bark:** Grey-green when young, with

A young Douglas Fir (*Pseudotsuga menziesii*).

many resin blisters, later dark and cracked. **Shoots:** Somewhat hairy, first light yellow then reddish-brown, later greybrown. **Needles:** 20–30 mm long, soft, flat, blunt to pointed in front, yellow-green to blue-green, two white stripes underneath; in two lines on young shoots, parted, otherwise growing around shoot; strongly scented when crushed. **Cones:** 5–10 cm long, cone scales are wide, round, smoothedged. Projecting bracts with long, narrow triangular tongue.

Typical close-packed long needles.

Scots Pine

Pinus sylvestris
Pine Family (*Pinaceae*)

The Scots Pine extends over a wide area, from the Pyrenees to central Europe, the Caucasus, central Siberia to the Amur region and as far north as Lapland. This wide spread is due partly to its adaptability – it grows both on gravelly-sandy and on marshy ground. The Scots Pine can live up to 300 years; owing to its strong root system with a long tap root, it is particularly wind-resistant. The wood is important as building material of all kinds and for chipboard and paper manufacture and not least as fuel; the resin of pines (and other conifers) is used to obtain turpentine and rosin. The tree is widely planted in forests, particularly on ground unsuitable for other forest trees. However, it is also planted in gardens and parks owing to its decorative shape, often reminiscent of Southern Parasol Pines. There are also some cultivars differing from type in size, shape and needle colour.

Growth: Up to 40 m high, initially conical, later widely projecting, almost umbrella-shaped. **Trunk:** Often bent when free-standing, or as forest tree with long straight trunk which has shed its lower branches. **Bark:** Dark-brown and cracked underneath, reddish in the branch region. **Shoots:** Greenish, later grey-brown, glabrous. **Needles:** In pairs, 4–8 cm long,

The Scots Pine (*Pinus sylvestris*).

tiff and pointed, growing close together, usually twisted and f semicircular cross-section, the flat side is usually grey-reen whereas the curved side is dark green. **Cones:** only 3–7 m long, with stalks, drooping, grey-brown and dull; cone-cales flat or slightly convex with blunt umbo; the cones fall fter a few years.

Mountain Pine
Pinus mugo
Pine Family (*Pinaceae*)

The Mountain Pine has a wide variety of shapes. Dependin
on its geographical habitat, the nature of the ground and th
altitude, it may be a low-lying bush (knee-high at the tre
limit) or a small, often multi-stemmed tree. It can also have
straight trunk with a generally conical habit. Correspondin
to these differences the species is sometimes divided into thre
sub-species. Another form, usually described as a separat
species, *Pinus uncinata*, may actually belong in the sam
species. It is tree-shaped and grows in South Germany on or a
the edge of high moors. The habitat of all these Mountai
Pines is the Alps, the Swiss Jura, the Black Forest, the Vosge
mountains, the Bohemian Forest, the Fichtelgebirge, th
Riesengebirge, the Erzgebirge, the Carpathians and th
Balkans, each region often producing its special varietie:
Mountain Pines grow both on chalk and on primitive rock a
altitudes up to 2500 m. Stands of dwarf Pines, which are ofte
impenetrable, serve an important purpose in high mountain:
they prevent erosion of slopes and protect from avalanche
Outside the mountains, the trees are frequently found i
gardens (rockeries). There are some garden varieties.

Growth: Low-lying or erect. (*P. uncinata* up to 20 m high
Trunk: Twisted in a curve or growing upright. **Bark:** Dar

Mountain Pine (*Pinus mugo*) in its natural habitat.

grey, rough, not flaking. **Shoots:** Glabrous, not pruinose. **Needles:** In pairs on a leaf sheath, 3–8 cm long, rigid, with blunt tip, green on both sides (slightly blue-green in *P. uncinata*), close-packed. **Cones:** Very variable, 2–7 cm long, round, egg-shaped or conical, with or without stalk, first green, later brown, often with sharp transverse ridge and thorn or hooked umbo.

Shoots and needles are similar on all Mountain Pines.

Austrian Pine
Pinus nigra
Pine Family (*Pinaceae*)

Owing to its geographical spread, the Austrian Pine ha formed numerous sub-species which are difficult to distin guish. Their production was favoured by the presence c isolated vegetation areas separated by wide spaces. Fo example the sub-species *Pinus nigra ssp. nigra* grows in Austri and the Western Balkans, *ssp. laricio* grows in Corsica, Soutl Italy and Sicily, *ssp. pallasiana* grows in Asia Minor, th Crimea and in the Caucasus, *ssp. salzmannii* grows in th Pyrenees area and *dalmatica* grows on the coast and th islands of North West Yugoslavia. Here we shall consider th representative sub-species *ssp. nigra*, the Austrian Black Pine It also occurs under the scientific names *Pinus nigra var austriaca*. The name 'black' (the Latin *nigra* means 'black' describes the generally sombre appearance of this Pine, due t the dark green needles and blackish bark. It is very undemanding and resistant and suitable eg for afforestation o dry, steep slopes, preferring limy soil. The wood is very rich ir resin and therefore insensitive to moisture. The Austrian Pin is the most important source of resin (turpentine) and can liv for up to 600 years.

Growth: 20–40 m high, egg-shaped, thicker above tha below, umbrella-shaped later. **Trunk:** Short; up-growing

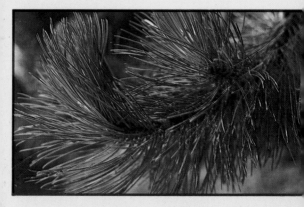

Austrian Pine (*Pinus nigra*). The lower part of the trunk is usually bare of branches.

thick branches. **Bark:** Black-brown and red-violet, with coarse long furrows and thick ridges, scaly. **Shoots:** Smooth, glabrous, first greenish, later yellow-brown or grey-brown. **Needles:** In pairs on a leaf-sheath, 8–15 cm long, rigid with prickly, often yellowish point, dark green. **Cones:** Up to 8 cm long, horizontal, without stalk, conical; scales with sharp transverse ridge and no thorn.

The outer shoots are bent upwards.

Arolla Pine
Pinus cembra
Pine Family (*Pinaceae*)

The Arolla Pine is native in Europe and Asia. In Europe i[t] grows in the Alps and Carpathians, where it usually occur[s] singly or in small groups at altitudes between 1200 and 2000 m. In Asia it grows in the Altai mountains and in larg[e] continuous stands between the Urals and Lake Baikal. I[t] prefers primitive rock, grows slowly and can live for up to 600 years. The yellowish, finely-fibred, tough wood is highl[y] valued for carving and turned work and for producin[g] furniture and soundboards of musical instruments. Th[e] Arolla Pine is rarely planted except in gardens and parks. I[n] course of time, therefore, the natural stands have progressive[-] ly shrunk because of the valuable wood. Single trees no[w] stand where there were forests a hundred years ago.

Growth: Up to 25 m high; the crown of older trees is ofte[n] multiple and wide (candelabrum). **Trunk:** Gnarled, thic[k] relative to its height. When free-standing the branches gro[w] down to the ground. **Bark:** First grey-green and smooth, late[r] black-brown and cracked. **Shoots:** Thick, covered with whit[e] to rusty yellow velvety hair, which later becomes dull **Needles:** In fives on each leaf sheath, 5–8 cm long, wit[h] triangular cross-section, dark green on outside, blue whit[e]

Arolla Pine (*Pinus cembra*) in a sheltered valley.

inside, in thick bunches particularly at ends of twigs. **Cones:** 5–8 cm long, grow only on very old trees. They are light cinnamon brown, with thick, wide scales. The seeds are nut-like and edible, and for this reason the fallen cones are often eaten by rodents.

Arolla Pines are easy to recognise from their groups of five needles.

Weymouth Pine
Pinus strobus
Pine Family (*Pinaceae*)

The Weymouth Pine with its soft, long, brightly shimmerin[g] needles and dense, towering growth is a particularly decora[c]tive tree and easily distinguished from most other pines. I[ts] habitat is eastern North America around the Great Lakes an[d] the New England States as far as Canada. It was named afte[r] Captain George Weymouth, R.N., who explored the coast [of] Maine at the beginning of the 17th century. The straight, lon[g] trunks became an important export product from this Britis[h] Colony; they were used to make masts. Meanwhile th[e] Weymouth Pine was also planted in Europe. In many parts [of] Europe it became a forest tree, owing to various advantageou[s] properties such as rapid growth, straight trunk and soft, onl[y] slightly shrinking wood (for cabinet-making and carving[)]. Above all, however, it is a valued park tree. Unfortunately, it i[s] easily attacked by blister rust. Healthy trees can live for mor[e] than 200 years. There are some garden varieties. *Strobus* from the Greek *strobos*, means 'whorl, twisted', and refers t[o] the spiral arrangement of cone scales.

Growth: Up to 50 m high, first conical, later broader. **Trunk** Straight; branches very long when old, in regular horizonta[l] whorls. **Bark:** Initially smooth, shining, grey-green, later dar[k]

Typical shape of an old Weymouth Pine (*Pinus strobus*).

brown with long cracks. **Shoots:** Thin, greenish, with fine hairs, later brown. **Needles:** In fives from one leaf sheath, 5–10 cm long, very thin, soft, straight, light green above, blue-white stripes on both sides underneath. **Cones:** Very large, 10–20 cm long, often somewhat bent (banana-shaped), first green then violet and brown in second year; cone-scales large and leathery, usually smeared with whitish dried resin. May be confused with the Bhutan Pine, *Pinus wallichiana* and the Macedonian Pine, *Pinus peuce* (page 78).

The thin, stiffly projecting needles are a distinctive feature.   71

Maritime Pine
Pinus pinaster
Pine Family (*Pinaceae*)

An important tree in the western Mediterranean area and the South European Atlantic coast: Italy, South France, Spain, Portugal. In these coastal regions the Maritime Pine is found in similar sites to the Aleppo Pine (page 74), and both trees are planted in forestry for binding the soil. The Maritime Pine also grows on sandy ground, dunes and rocky ground. It is relatively easy to recognise from its very long, rigid needles and very large and numerous cones, which are often grotesquely out of proportion to the size of the tree. For length of needles and cones, the Maritime Pine holds the record among original native European Pines. The wood is not very durable and is used for masts, thresholds, posts and paper manufacture. As with many other conifers, the resin is used to make turpentine, particularly in western France, where the Maritime Pine is planted mainly for this purpose. Oblique channels are cut in the bark of the trunk and the resin is collected as it runs out. Since the 16th century, the Maritime Pine has also been planted in the mild climate of southern England.

Growth: Up to 40 m high, but usually lower; loose, broad crown. **Trunk:** Often bent; branches in whorls, projecting

Young Maritime Pine (*Pinus pinaster*) with many cones.

horizontally; the lower part of the trunk is soon free of branches, even when free-standing. **Bark:** First light grey, later red-brown, thick and with deep cracks which divide it into square plates. **Shoots:** *Glabrous*, pale to reddish-brown, soon without needles at rear and with surface roughened by the remaining needle cushions. **Needles:** In pairs on a leaf sheath, up to 15 cm long thick, rigid and prickly, semi-circular cross-section, dark green. **Cones:** Up to 22 cm long, conical egg-shaped, light brown, shiny; the cone-scale umbo usually ends in a hook-like point; the cones remain many years on the tree, which is often crowded as a result.

branch with young and older cones.

Aleppo Pine
Pinus halepensis
Pine Family (*Pinaceae*)

The Aleppo Pine is found in the coastal Mediterranean region and on the hills and mountains of the adjacent country. It vegetation area extends from Spain to Asia Minor (the name i from the city of Aleppo in Syria). It is one of those Pines which after being noticed a few times, is always easy to recognise the 'cloudy' crown and the light whitish branches are th characteristic features of the Aleppo Pine together, on close inspection, with the typically-coloured cones. The tree is ver undemanding and hardy and well withstands the dryin coastal wind. It serves the important function of preventin erosion on hills and mountain slopes. Unfortunately, sma and larger stands are always in danger of forest fires, whic attack the highly-inflammable vegetation in the dry seasor Aleppo Pine resin is used to make turpentine and the wood i used for furniture and boats. Ships from Aleppo Pine wer made by the ancient Greeks. It is rare in Britain, but grown i a few places in the south.

Growth: Up to 15 m high, narrow in youth, wide and rounde later. **Trunk:** Often gnarled with crooked, twisted branche **Bark:** First silver-grey then reddish-brown; deep furrow when old; branches and twigs have light grey, almost whi

...lly-grown Aleppo Pine (*Pinus halepensis*) beside Mediterranean.

...ark. **Shoots:** Thin, greenish-brown or orange. **Needles:** In ...airs from a leaf sheath, up to 10 cm long, very thin, soft and ...exible, light green, in bunches at end of shoot. **Cones:** Up to ...0 cm long, on short thick bent stalks, pointed egg-shaped, ...iny red-brown with light grey umbos on cone scales, often ... threes; they remain on the tree for many years, which thus ...ecomes covered with cones of varying age.

...inus brutia is a similar species which is often classed as a sub-...ecies of the Aleppo Pine. It grows in the western Mediterra-...ean region. Its needles are longer (15 cm) and rigid. The ...ones are on straight stalks.

...anches with one and two-year cones. 75

Stone Pine
Pinus pinea
Pine Family (*Pinaceae*)

An extraordinarily decorative, picturesque tree which with i
umbrella-like crown is one of the characteristic plants on th
Mediterranean coast and Atlantic (Portugal). It grows ind
vidually in gardens and parks or in forest stands but alwa
near the coast, since it needs a mild moist climate. For th
reason, Stone Pines can also grow in Ireland and souther
England. The wood has less resin than other Pines and is use
for building and furniture. The seeds, Pine nuts, are edible ra
or roasted. Representations of the rounded, many-scaled pi
cone are known from the Assyrians, Greeks and Romans a
an artistic motif, often as an ornament on a well o
surmounting a building. In early Christianity the image of th
pine cone was used as a symbol for the Well of Life.

Growth: Up to 25 m high; with rounded crown when youn
umbrella-shaped when old. **Trunk:** Often fairly short, an
divided at a low height into a few thick branches, which the
spread horizontally. **Bark:** Reddish grey with long crack
later with large vertical plates which flake off and leave
reddish under-surface. **Shoots:** *Glabrous*, grey-green at firs
then brown. **Needles:** In pairs on a common leaf sheath, up
20 cm long, dark grey-green, sharply pointed; youn

one Pine (*Pinus pinea*) on Mediterranean coast.

ees have thinner, bluish needles. **Cones:** Thick and rounded,
to 14 cm long and 10 cm wide, brown and rather shiny;
e scales are rounded and convex, often with a sharp
ansverse ridge or a number of ridges extending radially from
e umbo and dividing the scale into six segments. The umbo
flat or projecting with a hook-like bend.

one Pines have long, stiff needles.

Bhutan Pine
Pinus wallichiana
Pine Family (*Pinaceae*)

The soft, drooping needles of the Bhutan Pine are its typic feature. Otherwise it might be confused with a youngis Weymouth Pine, which like it has large cones and groups five needles. This particularly decorative tree comes from th Himalayas, where it grows at altitudes between 2000 an 4000 m and forms thick forests with other conifers. It is four in our parks and gardens, not only in the mild Mediterranea climate but also in central Europe and Britain. It wa introduced here in 1823. The Latin name honours th Danish-English botanist Wallich, who was active mainly India at the beginning of the 19th century. The Bhutan Pir can live for 150 years. It is being grown in forestry.

Growth: Height up to 30 m, tight and conical in youth, lat with loose crown. **Trunk:** Lower part without branches older trees. **Bark:** Initially smooth, dark grey, later cracke coming off in thin plates. **Shoots:** Glabrous, light green, lat brown-yellow. **Needles:** In fives on one leaf sheath, 10–18 c long, very thin, extending forwards at end of twig, otherwi drooping, white-green, triangular cross-section. **Cones:** 1 30 cm long, slightly curved, covered with resin, initial white-purple red, later light brown. Cone scales long, wri

...wo closely adjoining Bhutan Pines (*Pinus wallichiana*).

...ed, somewhat thickened. Bhutan Pine can be confused not ...ly with Weymouth Pine (*P. strobus*) but also with the **...acedonian Pine** (*P. peuce*). This is native to Yugoslavia, ...bania and Bulgaria and is cultivated in our country as a ...corative garden and park tree. The needles of *P. peuce* are ...orter; 10 cm long, stiff and not drooping. The cones are only ...-12 cm long, but otherwise similar to those of Bhutan or ...eymouth Pine. The cone scales are wrinkled and furrowed.

...pical very thin needles, some loosely drooping.

Index

Total: 94

Foreword

'What conifer is that?' This question can quickly be answered on the spot, using this tree identification book. This book contains pictures and descriptions of all the most common conifers in Europe. These are not only the originally native European species but also the non-European trees which have been planted in our latitudes in the course of time. They come mainly from the temperate zones of North America and Asia.

The 70 colour photos and 50 drawings, specially prepared for this book, give the general appearance of the tree and important details regarding branches, needles and cones. Concise, easily-understood text describes the shape, bark, shoots, needles and cones or fruit. The nature-lover will also learn the most important facts about origin, spread, habitat, use in forestry and as timber.

The species in this guide occur in forests and countryside and also in parks or gardens, where one is particularly likely to come across the numerous garden varieties or 'cultivars', which often differ considerably from the type, which has the characteristics of the species.

In the garden we find dwarf, pyramidal, columnar, creeping or drooping forms with blue, silver or yellow needles, so that it is sometimes difficult even for the expert, let alone the layman, to identify which tree has provided the origin of a particular form. If we remember, for example, that there are about 130 garden varieties of Lawson's Cypress (*Chamaecyparis lawsoniana*), it will be clear why this book is deliberately restricted to typical varieties.

In this connection, a word on names and classification of conifers. Every amateur botanist will soon find that without scientific names we cannot get an overall view, because terms in English and other languages result only in utter confusion. One prominent example is the name Fir, which has to cover all kinds of trees having evergreen needles. Cedar and Cypress are other favourite terms which are often used inaccurately. They occur in botanical books, but only because they have been around for so long; they date from the time before systematic botanical nomenclature.

Every plant and every tree has a scientific name made up of two words, usually Latin or Greek. For example the Colorado Spruce is called *Picea pungens*. *Picea* is the generic name and means Spruce, whereas *pungens* denotes the species and means prickly.

In addition to its most important function (of being a practical aid to identification), this guide provides much of interest about the special features of the various conifers – information not to be found in any other tree identification book.

The more we know about the things of the natural world, the more we shall understand and love it.

Georg Zauner

The author:

Georg Zauner, born in Germany in 1920, painter and graphic artist, subsequently author and director of numerous popular scientific films and prize-winning TV films.

Scientific advice and collaboration:

Professor Dr Peter Schütt, Head of the Institute of Forest Botany, University of Munich.